This little book is dedicated to:

_____

You are the one

that knows me the

best.

I don't have to worry,

have never a care,

for the rest of

my life,

you'll always be

there.

Romances
fade, but
you and I
will
always
remain.

We've been

so good

with our

promises

to

each

other.

A

confidant

is a

commodity

beyond

measure.

So

fortunate,

we are,

to have

each other.

You and I share qualities in quantity.

Our individual voices

are something to write home

about,

yet we sing together

in great

harmony.

You know what

hurts me...

you keep me from it.

It is a mutual

service.

*I am so **happy***

to know...

that you'll always
be there for me!

Acquaintances

come and go, but

you will always

be my best buddy.

You make my

life

richer

by just

being you!

When I'm down,
I call you,
and I feel better.

Sorry you're down.

Now it's

your turn...

Through
all,
'
we've been
fast friends.

*You don't
always have to
be profound,
you just have
to be
around.*

*Ours will
always be
the model
for*
lasting
relationships.

We share a spoon,
a glance, a smile,
and we've said more...

than most people do

in an entire

day.

During my
trials and
flights
you share
the burden
and relief.

When we are older, we sure will have fun thinking about all the mischief we've done!

You

are

a pack

of

blessings.

We play
and grow
and learn
together.

You keep me sane,
my friend,
yet keep me in my
dreams.

We hope for

love,

we wish for

success,

for ourselves

and

for each other.

*If we
were bees,
'd hang out
at the
same flower!*

You're my pal,
my sounding board,
my little voice of
reason,
the little devil
on my shoulder!

Even though we
might not speak often,
when we do,

we never seem to

lose touch.

Rail
Pass

TICKET
★ Cruise

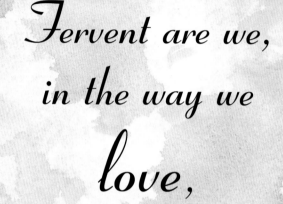

Fervent are we,
in the way we
love,
in the way we
live,

in the way

we

are

friends.

Listen friend, to me,
we've survived them
all so far,
this, too, will pass.

Our friendship

flows

like

India ink!

I tell you

every day,

but it just is

not enough...

you are

reverently

valuable

to me!

...may
we
always
be
friends...